Chronicles Of A Tin Woman

Lyfe Publishing – July 2018

Vanessa Rainey Johnson tirelessly works to bring awareness to the growing problem of suicides in our community. She is committed to donating ten percent of all sales of The Chronicles of a Tin Woman to her non-profit organization, Blue Moon 211 Inc.

Blue Moon 211 Inc. Program Description

Blue Moon 211 Inc. is a Suicide Awareness/Prevention and Intervention organization. We provide training, resources and referrals in community-based suicide prevention, intervention and postvention services. Services are designed to assist individuals, public and private entities such as Mental Health/Public Health Authorities, Schools, Counties, Community Coalitions, Law Enforcement and Private Organizations who are interested in developing suicide alertness.

This organization works closely with all entities, to ensure program efficiency is provide in this sensitive area of life and in reducing the risk of suicide events. Our training is provided by the American Foundation for Suicide Prevention (AFSP), Living Works Inc., the Crisis Center of Tampa Bay and the Crisis Text line.

Mission Statement

Our mission is to bring awareness/prevention by means of educational materials, speaking engagements, as a referral/resource center and to improve the overall mental health of individuals in the community.

Vision

Our vision is to reach out to the communities through determination and dedication helping save lives inspiring peace and making a difference in the world.

WHO IS A TIN WOMAN

She looks up toward the sky and cries out, "God where are you?" She knows God is the author and finisher of her faith. Oh, what a mighty God she serves, knowing, if she allows God to handle her needs, she can make it to another day. Life has a way of knocking us off balance. She remains steadfast in her faith; she can conquer if she learns how to master the task.

Every day brings forth a new beginning to start over with a different perspective. Her eyes, at times, become gloomy with worries, not really understanding life is a journey. On the journey, there will be a bump, dead end, curve, another path, a cliff and a straight road; making a choice is sometimes difficult. The challenge is sometimes too much to bear; however, she lifts her head up with pride, swallows, takes a deep breath and continues along the journey. She is a "Tin Woman" because she takes control of the heaviness from her past so she can live in freedom toward her future. Rock the world, my love. You have made it across the valley. It's now time to climb the terrains of the mountain.

TIN WOMAN

The foundation of a woman was not built to be broken; she must continue to rise without any residue. One must realize underneath the exterior is a woman of heart. Yes, she has been called "a woman of strength and courage." She is a woman taken for granted, dehumanized, sexualized and criticized. The more she gives, the more her love is taken for granted; it is taken away, stripped from her soul.

She never stops caring for her love ones. Even after her bones are brittle and dry, there is work to be done. She is not robotic. She deserves to be loved from a sincere heart, not with a superficial, demeaning love.

Recognize her power, appreciate her mind and trust in her spirit. She is the Tin Woman with a heart.

The Journey Begins

As the skies opened, welcoming my arrival, I escaped the shadows of darkness. Looking in my rearview mirror of life, I rejoiced with scared joy. I was embarking on a new future; however, I was afraid of my past.

Running away from the pain, I slipped into a hole, a hole so deep only God could help me escape. Fallen from the sky in the chaos of life,

I had to find me. I had to let go even if it meant losing me. I had to do it now! I was worn out from everyone's labeling. Their words touched a soft spot in my ear. "You are strong." "Oh, you can handle it." "I admire you." "That is the way life is."

As I continued to hear these words echoing in my black space, the more I sunk deeper into a slum. This is the hole I dug, that same hole would be a stepping stone to my stability. I was always told, "What goes on in your house, stays in your house," Don't allow the right hand to know what the left hand is doing" and "A happy home is one where everyone else stays out."

No one ever explained these jargons and we dared not ask because "Closed mouths do not get you fed" or "You may out talk yourself; therefore, stay in a child's place." We did as we were told. We grew up with the stigma of abuse and fear.

The moment I began to sink, I could not stop my spiritual, physical or mental stability from spinning out of control. I remember that old merry-go-round as a child. I heard the laughs as it spun out of control. I screamed; no one heard me. I cried; my tears blew in the wind. I wanted off; it was spinning too fast for me to jump. I was dizzy; my heart skipped a beat. I jumped off that old spinning mechanism and fell on a broken bottle.

Lying in a pool of blood, I was unable to move. I waited for someone to help me. Instead, they laughed. I got up and limped home, crying tears of devastation. My mother nurtured my surface wounds and said, "Big girls do not cry." She was trying to make me strong; however, she was unknowingly diffusing my pain; "tough love."

I carried those words with me into adulthood. I lived without living, the air I breathed was toxic and the pain I felt was a pain of numbness without description; only experience.

Tin Woman, where are you? You have the attributes of a queen. You are radiant, elegant, victorious, merciful, compassionate, empowering, angelic, fiery, divine and genuine.

You adorn your layers with the exquisite colors of the world: silver, bronze, blue, white, green, black, gold, red, gray and lavender. Stand up and cheer. You are the star of the show, deserving the joyfulness. It is your time.

This short story is dedicated to the Tin Women in the world and to my daughters, Nephthys, Nefertiti and Neferteri. Life has left you with many scars. I anoint your heads with the oils from our ancestors. May their oils continue to lubricate your most delicate parts, to pull each generation to the next level. Pull, rise, spread and soar; keep the momentum, allow the rivers of strength to flow into eternality.

To my sons, Osiris and Horus, recognized the strength, nurture her spirit, giving her warmth, compassion and appreciative love. Allow your queen room to grow; she will forever respect and genuinely love you.
Teach her the attributes of life to withstand the storms. She is your chi (life-force), you are her yang (energy). Together you can conquer and devour because through Christ all things are possible (Philippians 4:13).

"Out of her ashes, she rises, without any residue left behind."

In loving memory of Lottie Flemming Rainey Bender (mother), may her spirit of strength rest on the shoulders of her generation.

I Am Woman

Come take a walk with me. There is
Something I would like you to see.
We are going to walk inside of my mind.
There are a lot of good things you
Will find. I am a woman who likes
Nice things, all the riches life has
To bring. Respect this mind; it's one of a kind.

I am a woman who looks for understanding.
I'm sweet by nature and not too demanding.
I like my man to be sensitive to my needs,
Sometimes I like for him to beg and say please.
Respect this mind; it's one of a kind.

I am a strong black woman.
I am a queen in this land.
I will walk by my man's side.
I will let him take control and be
My guide. Respect this mind; it's one of a kind.

I am a woman who loves to be loved.
My heart is pure like the color of
A dove. Faith and God are what i believe,
Joy and a peace of mind are what i receive.
Respect this mind; it's one of a kind.

1 - RADIANCE

She is a woman of substance intermingling with the toxicity of love, forgiveness and joy. You never know the quality of a woman who has suffered many scars along the freeway of life.

Broken, battered, confused and used, she continues to move smoothly with grace as if the spirit of a warrior has descended upon her soul.

Held together with the gravity of love, she rises above all things slicing away at her heart. We can picture her presence in our thoughts as the strength of a lioness and the spirit of a dove. Her soul is filled with the wisdom of Seshat and the beauty of the moon that shines boldly in the dark, illuminating the sky.

Radiance, we must say! Her outer layer is metallic silver, yet her heart bleeds for mercy of the lives she loves. She carries her burdens as if one could sit on a cloud, absorbing its sweet mist falling into the coolness of the land.
Emphatically she laughs like a soothing chime of a harp, methodically striking a chord in harmony with the harpist. Courageous enough to endure the struggle and sassy enough to enjoy her journey.

Liberated in a world where beauty goes beneath the surface, yet she mourns for the company of another with an unspoken whisper.

Yes, we can assume this magnificent character has no boundaries when it comes to the harshness of her soul. While others are sleeping, she is brazening her layers with an oil which is not just an ordinary oil.

This sweet oil will give her the lubrication needed to conquer the impossible in spite of her tears, fears and tribulations.

Radiance is her name. She continues to allow her diamond-coated, undying love to discharge into the heart of others.

Mystical Gem

My Queen, you are a mystical gem all the colors combined as one. As I follow the rainbow for my pot of gold. I can trace true love coming from your soul. Shimming, gleaming like the twinkling of the stars, I can feel my light shining near and far.

Rich in spirit and truth, was instilled in you to me.... From our ancestors we were told to pull and push, you would be my ram standing quietly in the bush. I love you for your patience understanding and wisdom. You gave me much joy, I love your charisma.

When I cry, you weep from the depths of your heart; I do not take it for granted, it was genuine from the start. When I'm far away in distress, our spirit connects as one; it would be that way, from years to come. Through your eyes, I see hope, your heart of gem gives me the strength to cope.

2 - ELEGANCE

How profound is her nature as she thinks about ways to care for her family. Most would say, "She is brave." However, she cries from the depths of a heart that rips away the clutter, placing it in the center for a keepsake.

The uniqueness of her attributes is found in the mystical hourglass of time, time that goes unrecorded in the minds of her predators.

She is simple, yet classy. Holding her head high, she walks with tidiness. Sophisticatedly, she maneuvers in a world of men, tasting the savoring favor of honey as she succeeds in purpose.

Elegant as a jewel, laced with bronze for her outer layer. Her layer shines as if the sun has ascended into the heavenly skies, splashing its existence with rays of colors.

Refined and dignified, she displays her demeanor in the most polishing moments of her life. There has been no other Tin Woman before her, and no other after her; who can obtain her diplomacy.

Peacefully, she lives her life in a chaotic pile of desperateness. Shattering into discord, she began to crack; yet, somehow, the pieces remained whole.

Boldly, she wears her mask of colors for the world to praise; sparkling with gems, refined copper, and hues of fuchsia, blue, coral, emerald green, red and tangerine.

She is elegant, the perfect display of a virtuous woman flowing into the river of eternity.

She marks her path with control. Paint the picture or does one allow the picture to paint itself?

She does not fully understand why man would not want to symbolize life as being a vessel, a temporary solution to a holistic home

Painting the Picture

As we watch the moon illuminating the sky, casting off its' reflection in the water below. The feel of the night air breeze as it blows across our face while we stand holding hands in the stillness of the night gazing into each other eyes feeling a feeling that has never been felt before, painting a picture of a love that we share.

We forget about the turmoil's and the tribulations, we forget about the pain of yesterday; we do not live for tomorrow only for the moment. God has listened to our cries of understanding, our desires of needing; he has blessed us with each other, while two hearts intertwine into one, just for the moment.

Our love has surpassed the feeling that we have denied ourselves, running…, running from a love that we so badly need. The mask has become unveil, no more pretense, no more games, just feeling each other for the moment, letting the picture paint itself not painting the picture.

3 - VICTORIOUS

She has been called an opportunist, but only if the opportunity fit the occasion for a positive outcome.

Victory is in the spirit of those who believe they can achieve with maximization within their power.

She believes, "all things are possible, through Christ who gives us strength" (Philippines 4:13).

This Tin Woman proclaims victory as she wears her swords, shield and buckler. Standing tall like a giraffe, she gazes with alertness over her loved one.

Stripped of her pride, she wears blinders, closing out the glowing light that once shined in her eyes. She is victorious because she dances in a rhythmic beat while the flames consume her spirit. The moment the fire starts to burn deep in her spirit, she kneels before God.

"Burn, as you must; however, I am not alone in this furnace," she cries out. She does not see herself as a victim, although life has battered her like a raging ocean during the storm.

Victorious wears the metallic color of blue. This brilliant woman can sustain the rustiness of her outer layer. However, she continues to shine.

She is strong, protected and vibrant. Her blue color sets the tone for peace, confidence, loyalty, trust, wisdom and faith. She rules the nation with the tip of her sword and a twelve-star crown. Her metallic color is valuable to mankind. She is a blessed woman because she is Victorious.

I Can Feel You

I can feel your present even though you are not here; I can feel your touch when you are near. I know that in my heart you hold the key, I can feel you, I know you feel me.

Baby our beginning is for the present, past and the future; our feelings are not different nor or they nurture. Your voice, your smile that twinkle in your eye; shines in my heart, like the sun in the sky.

A breath of fresh air is what I feel you see; you are the one God has given to me. Baby, what I feel is love; you are embedded in my mind, heart, body and soul; a new life is about to unfold, Baby I can feel you.

4 - MERCIFUL

God created this woman as a sacrificial lamb. Little did she know that she would sacrifice her freedom to care for those within her family circle.

Through turmoil, sweat and tears, she continues to nurture without taking the time to breathe the crispiness of the morning air.

Her labor is threatening, overwhelming and vicious; however, she maintains her charisma. She is reminded, "Forgiveness is for your soul, not the other person." These words sometimes cause her to stumble with stubbornness as she feels the pain piercing her heart.

Merciful as she tries to recollect what caused this dilemma in her life. Sometimes, she questions the authenticity of the creator. Yet, in her questioning, she is aware everything in life happens for a reason; in her season she will defeat the odds.

This woman of compassion knows that she can walk the path of peace and healing if she'll just "let go." She arms herself with knowledge, understanding if she looks back on her problems, her spirit will convert into bitterness; her heart will become hard.

Merciful is fruitful with the metallic layer of white. White signifies purity, balance, value and transparency.

She appreciates the yin and yang of life because the glittering of the stars tells her she has the power. If she can see white (light), everything else is visible. The light will give her hope, and hope will give her the endurance to be merciful, forgiving and loving.

A God Sent Friend

An everlasting friend is truly hard to find; a God send friend is one of a kind. You are very special to me; in my heart you hold a different key. The key you hold open many doors; the door to my soul, no one can go.

You listen to my most inner thoughts; when there is no one else to be sought. You do not judge me for my right nor wrong; you give me strength to help me become strong. God places people in our lives at different times, in different places, different seasons and for different reasons.

You were placed in my life to show me the way; you have given me hope day by day. A God send friend you are to me; you opened my eyes and set my mind free. Thank you for always being there; it feels good, to let me know you care.

5 - COMPASSIONATE

Oh, the beauty of a compassionate woman who loves deeply. This woman's tears flood the streams of life with teardrops from heaven due to the overflow of blessings.

A woman of worthiness inhales and exhales her rights. She knows she is valuable. She stays with her truth, knowing that her past does not define her future.

Compassionate from the beginning of time, floating in and out as she escalates to the top; grasping for the hand of another woman to surpass her vision.

Marked with the kiss of an angel, she wears her crown with sensitivity. Her desire to make things better for others is loyal. She is human; yet, her somatic spirit appeases the heart of the most uncaring soul.

This woman's venom can be poisonous as a protective mechanism when she has her back against the wall. However, her soft-hearted spirit makes way for all to embrace her tenderness with loving care. She has little to no complicity, her metallic layer is green. Green is the symbol of peace and life.

In every season, there is time to plan, wait and activate. It will change in the blink of an eye. She is given the attribute of patience to know when it's her time and; in this time, she waits.

Full of spirit, she moves at the beckoning of her internal voice, blocking out the external sounds of a busy environment. Her humbleness brings forth meekness as she lives her life with joyfulness.

The aroma of jasmine, sprigs of myrtle and lily of the valley are a natural fragrance that purifies her casing, allowing her armor to glow under intense forces. She will walk through the valley while allowing her compassionate nature to charm the breeze of the midnight air.

I am a woman on a solid rock. I stand, holding the world on my shoulders, swaying to the rhythmic beat of agony. I will not bow. I will walk with true confidence. I have patience because I know God will do great things for those who wait (Psalms 91).

I am the butterfly waiting for birth. I have gone through sanctification, transformation, termination, identification and renewed foundation. Now, I can celebrate my salvation.

I am a woman of strength (1 Timothy 1:12), compassion, discipline, faith, love, forgiveness and wisdom (Proverbs 1:20).

I can envision and anticipate my blessing; it's only a stepping stone away. This Tin Woman's compassion brings forth a new spirit of freedom, the spirit of a butterfly as she pledges to herself and to the universe.

Butter Fly

I pledge to love myself for whom I am.
I understand I have faults and flaws.
I am beautiful, unique and victorious.
I will not give up on life.
I forgive you and I forgive me.
I will seek help when I am in distress.
I am in harmony and peace with my spirit

6 - EMPOWERED

She empowers the weak and infuses the strong.

Acceptance is the word she uses to allow her blessings to connect. This Tin Woman is proud. She puts on a brave face, but the truth is she feels everything very deeply.

She can hide her pain but not her anger, especially when someone attacks her loved ones or abuses her trust. She loves more than anyone can ever imagine.

This magnitude of a woman meets people where they are. She does not look down on others. Instead, she cultivates their gift, allowing judgment to pass over her flaws so she will not see their flaws. She follows their conversation and actively listens to their needs with a pure smile; she nods.

Sister, I am your keeper. I am your keeper because I have been kept. I will help navigate you along your path. God will order your steps; you have the power to move forward or stay still.

Her generous heart gives her the ability to pray for her enemies in conflict, even when her mind says, "No way!" She is a motivator, stimulator and change maker. She is a woman on a mission. However, she understands she cannot do it alone.

This beauty wears the metallic color of black. She is powerful in every aspect of life. She has an I-can-I-will-do spirit to see any project to completion. She is not afraid to receive or help others; she is not intimated.

Forgetting her own needs, she gives uncompromisingly with all her heart and soul, sometimes if not all the time. Black is strong, brave and powerful. She has the power and she knows her power!

Dreams

There is no secret, in what you can do; I thought it was, I found out it is so true. Strive further than you can see; put your mind to it and be all you can be. Your destiny has been set from birth; your mother gave you life, God was there first. You are a Queen on this land; hold your head high, never look down on man.

Dream of succeeding as you grow up; success is made through determination, it's not based on luck. Wish upon a star is what was told to me; follow your dreams, they hold the key. Dream of being strong, smart and rich; the world is in your hands, don't you dare quit. Have faith and trust in God's word because in us God lives, in God we serve.

7 - ANGELIC

Can you see her halo? Do you feel her love?

She is one of God's most caring, nurturing creature. She flows into time with the wings on her back. Her spirit keeps her ageless; her attitude keeps her phenomenal. Yes, she is the chosen one to bring forth life to cultivate this land.

Woman, she was called from the beginning of time; she upholds all of mankind. Her wisdom and insights surpass any creature on this earth.

She was formed out of the rib of a man, to be his helper, support and queen. She wears her crown, high upon her head.

Gold is this phenomenal woman's metallic color. Rich in supplication, worthy to bear the burdens of her family.

Gold, what men cannot do without. She is royal, bodacious and walks with polish. Though broken, battered and beaten, she continues to rise with the gravity beneath her feet.

Gold, I give to you, for the rewards you deserve. This Tin woman of gold never asks for anything, yet is deserving of everything.

Although she is humble, she bears the stripes of a tigress. This species is one-of-a-kind; no two fingerprints are alike.

Gold is the color of the sun, the giver of life that shines brightly from the sky. A woman of status due to her the glow that enriches her aroma.

Angelic magic and exotic, she sparkles as she lights the path for man. As valuable as the air we breathe, bringing life from the rays of her most romantic passageway.

Faith

It is a blessing to know that you are in God's care.
God will shower you in his love, you will know that God is there.

God will pull you out of the water when you are in too deep, God will wipe away your tears when you decide to weep. You see, the pain you feel is only temporary, give it all to God, you will be in his sanctuary.

The love of God is an unconditional love, it is pure like a baby, gentle as a dove. Learning to love you is the most important love of all, this will teach you to love another you will never fall.

Faith is the key to your peace, you will be blessed with God's riches, even as you sleep. When you have awakened, there will be a glow on face. Look up and smile, you are in God's grace.

8 - FIERY

She loves a hot, passionate and an on-time love. Her heart floats in her most inner being, the lava from within begins to stir and erupts like a volcano.

Fiery red is her heart because it pumps away her pleasure, love and compassionate nature. The love this Tin Woman craves and possesses is displayed through her actions, her forgiving and giving spirit.

The metallic color of red can mean danger due to a cracked heart; bleeding immensely, stealing the pride of a scorn; yet, she is a determined woman.

She lives for her family. She will do anything necessary to ensure they are protected and safe.

A wife, mother, lover and caregiver to the world, she holds this color well without any regrets. The fire burns deep down in her soul, undertaking the scrutiny of her world.

Her desire continues to give her energy as she tosses the fiery ball towards anyone who attacks her character.

She understands the blood. She knows the sweat which tickles down her face, moisturizing her skin as it creeps from her pores.

Red creates its own skills; it must be used with caution.

Red can bring forth life and red can take life away. The brightness of this color is vivacious.

Red depends on what experience is impacting her life on any day.

This Tin Woman of red stands with strength and will-power, making her point obvious to those who are listening. She is efficient, can be domineering; however, she is dynamic. Go ahead and try this fiery woman.

She will give you everything you need from the core of her heart. The moment she feels love, she traces love, allowing her hand to penetrate through a glass corridor of the heart of her enemy. It is captivating to know you are loved by this woman.

Black Rose

Pretty was the rose given to me, beauty was the picture I held dear to my heart. The sweetness of its aroma intoxicated my mind; it lingered for days to come, until I ran out of time.

I never knew something that smelled so sweet could be so deadly; however; I accepted the gift with joy and pride. Inhaling the pleasantness of its scent, I was consumed with its beauty not realizing the stint. A picture-perfect scene made in hell; I walked unprotected into the devil's cell.

Captivated by the color not seeing the thorns nor caring of the pains; I was caught up in the moment, feeling the sensual healing game. In an instant, the fluids deteriorated my body and corrupted my soul, I knew I was dying young, I would never live to be old.

While the petals began to fall, as did my life; I drift deeper into sleep while my spirit slipped away, my God I felt weak. I cried out to the Heavens "God release me from my distress", Lord knows all I wanted to do is rest; while the Rose became Black.

9 - DIVINE

She was born to be divine; however, her spirit was manifested into a world of corruption. Yes, this woman breathed life with the most powerful force of the universe. She screamed with joy, agony and love as she entered a world unlike what she had become accustomed to while surrounded by the water of her mother's womb.

Sweet, soft and gentle was her nature until the corruptions of the world embarked into her heart. Her illusions are natural, bringing forth many colors combined. However, this Tin Woman represents the metallic color gray.

Divine, a spirt to surpass all because she is the mother of the universe. Her Orisha attracts. It is undermined by many, her spiritual overshadows and her physical strength.

She guides others with powerful affirmations, bringing forth the best of their abilities to cope with life.

Gray is not a color of gloom; it is a philosophical color that surrounds thought. This Tin Woman thinks about her next move as she journeys through life. The earth obeys her wakening spirit as she mourns deeply with remorse for the loss of loved ones. The sounds echo from heaven as the skies force teardrops. God hears her tears, sorrows and pains. God weeps with and for her.

This Tin woman is intriguing, deeply rooted in her world because she exists not by the confinements of others but due to her survival nature. Her mood can be smoky or light gray. It depends on the circumstances. Yes, her decision-making can be indecisive; yet, she is practical in her thought process.

To battle the negative forces, she must drain her soul of the waste with meditation/prayer, bringing justice to her essence.

Gray, a color of neutrality, she listens with calmness; yet, hears with clarity. There is no loss in this color because she is a mysterious being with sophistication, balance and timeless love.

Paradise

When one feels love, it's within reach. Close your eyes, the memories are like a movie pending, not wanting to let go of the image. The scent of a sweet fragrance, only you can smell lingers. Without hesitation, the scent makes you want to hold, touch, feel and create the sensation of ecstasy; as you float in an outer body experience, your mind reaches its destiny.

Hearing the soft melody as the sensual sound forms in your thoughts; creating a warm feeling in your heart a yearning to be sought. Oh, the beauty of the sound as we connect, in spirit, heart and soul; God knew from the beginning, we were meant to be in one mold.

We love, adore and appreciate the greatness gift God has given to mankind. When I look into the eyes of your soul, love unravels in my heart, sweeping my inner existence into a land of no return, baby, we have nothing but time......Love is paradise in the eyes of the beholder.

10 - GENUINE

Genuine, the essence of love. Snap, crackle and pop; she can keep it real through the pain. As the pressure of her walls collapse, she knelt to pick up the broken pieces.

This Tin Woman takes those pieces and begins to build. She works day and night, thinking of creative ways to overcome. She does not see herself as a victim; she understands life sometimes knocks her down to get back up for her grand finale. Her day will arrive. She will wear her crown of glory because she deserves all life has to offer.

Stripped away, underneath her struggling soul, you will find the most exotic color of the universe, lavender.

Lavender, feel her spirit, see her vibes and love her style. She is every Tin Woman. The freshness of the scent blends with every natural fragrance God created. Yes, she is ordinary. She is a woman with healing power, releasing in the atmosphere her essential oils.

This Genuine flower was created to cherish the land with all she should give. During her enduring times, she perseveres. She rises while she blows lightly in the wind.

She is the lotus, floating in the wishing well without a root as it flourishes. Electrifying, rejuvenating and stimulating this land, she continues to give, uplift and forgive from her sacred place.
Eternal love is her story. Her delicate nature tells it all.

Her metallic tin will not let her fall. She is historical, spiritual and possesses uniqueness; she is a symbol of devotion.

Lavender, the richness of a quintessential woman, precious sweet and explicitly loved.

Go tell your story, tell your story on God's time. Only you can write your life story; only you can sing your song.

Power

*F*aith is holding onto God's unchanging hands when all hope is gone. Our feelings of tomor row bring forth sorrow; he will wipe away our tears and take away our fears. God closes one door so that we can walk through another. Blessing overflow when you listen to your mother.

God is our comfort in need and God is our friend in refugee. As we walk this journey of life, we believe that our days are forever. We live life without a care, seeking happiness, pleasure and joy everywhere. We call on God only when we are in need, not opening our heart to receive. Have faith in his word, in his word, there is love; in his love, there is power to help us in every hour. God has wonder-working power. BELIEVE.

11 - RARE JEWEL

"Underneath the metal exterior is a warm, secure little girl, waiting to discover her true identity. She sees in you what you do not see in yourself. While she is discovering who you are, she will come to know her beauty."

She is not a being of habit, she floats in and out of her emotions. Yes, she is a stellar who can take one to the mountains and glide you gently to the valley. She is rare, she was created to be, all anyone would want her to be. Touch her heart gently with strokes of love, you will galvanize her joy. Her aroma signifies a peachy smell, as her façade flows like the torrents of a waterfall.

She silently waits while she simmers her desire to strike against the odds. This woman knows the odds very well, for she has lived through many with grace. In her garden, she cultivates the fruits of her spirit, making sure they become ripe in her season.

Her peachy metallic signifies her virginity, transparency, youthfulness and immortality. She is the "Tree of Life" without her, life will not exist; therefore, one must be mindful of what is said against her, she is the root.

This rare jewel of Carnelian, Malachite, Amethyst, Sapphires and Emeralds sparkles at a glimpse because her wisdom is a treasure chest of keepsakes.

She breaks disharmony while promoting balance, positivity, transformation, confidence and unity. She is the only creation of God who were created to uplift man.

The gates of heaven open as this Tin Woman enter into her own, not taking anything for granted but allowing herself to be humble in all she possess. She is a rare jewel, she can be polished or in dust;yet, this piece of mineral will shine.

Seasons

Heavens beckons your call, God knew you would not fall; determine in your purpose, specific with your ambitious, faithful in your action; God created you, to become the main attraction.
Allow your hands to open, you cannot receive your blessing with a full hand;
take the center of the stage and make a grand stand.

Yes, you have lived in the valley of residue; sexual assault, date rape, suicide attempt, sexism, divorce, racism, unruly children, victim of domestic violence, bullied and homelessness. However, you continue to smile, showing God gratitude.

A victorious woman (Proverb 31) you are called, as you walk
with pride;
knowing your past trails, was the devils ride; however, you con-
tinue to strive.

God took you from the rubbish and made a meal for a queen;
giving you back life, this strengthen your self-esteem.
It's your season to soar across the nations of this land;
Stand tall with grace, you are a Tin Woman.

Vanessa Rainey Johnson

Vanessa R. Johnson received her Associate Degree from Hillsborough Community College Liberal Arts and her Bachelor's Degree in Psychology and Sociology from University of Tampa. She graduated in September 2018 with a Master's degree in Christian Counseling.

She will start her journey in pursing her Doctoral degree in Philosophy with an emphasis in Performance Psychology from Grand Canyon University.

She currently holds certifications in Cosmetology, Life Insurance, Pre-license in Real Estate, Safe Talk T4T trainer, ASIST trained (Applied Suicide Intervention Skills Trained), and Peer Educator for Diabetes. She is also a Crisis Counselor.

She is a member of the Health Equity Champions Committee at Navicent Health Hospital and participates as a board member for the local recreation center in Georgia.

Ms. Johnson is a Tai Chi instructor and she teaches coping skills and meditation at the local recreation center.

In 2013, she founded Blue Moon 211 Inc. Suicide Awareness/Prevention Organization. In April 2015, a second chapter was organized in Middle Georgia.

In July 2015, Mrs. Johnson formed an organization that empowers youths, The International Youth Empowerment Coalition Task Force. She loves working with people and teaching others about hope, faith and productivity to achieve the abundance of life.

Blue Moon 211 Inc. has several committees to help in areas of domestic violence, homelessness, veteran's affairs and bullying.

In July 2013, 2014 and 2015, she traveled on missionary trips to Montego, Jamaica, St. James Parrish; this is where she had the opportunity to do her first overseas workshops on Suicide Prevention.

In 2014/15, with other suicide prevention organizations, she traveled to Washington, DC, to speak to members of Congress on Mental Health/Suicide.

In 2014-2016 she advocated in Tallahassee, the state capital of Florida. In 2017/18, she advocated at the Georgia state capital.

She is married to Johnny Johnson, a mother of five grown children and a grandmother of 11.

A Word From
Vanessa Rainey-Johnson

My purpose is to help lead all people on the right path to better living by knowing God, living a Godly life and sharing knowledge with others. Knowledge is power and my slogan is "No Peace, No Power." Without these, you will live a life in the dark. My educational endeavors will help me be a better advocate for others. As I help others, I will continue to grow spiritually.

If you ever find yourself falling into a deep hole, moving through a tunnel without lights or feel as if your ship is sinking, remember to hold on and seek help. You are never alone. Call the National Suicide Prevention Crisis Line at 800-273-TALK (8255) or text the National Crisis Text line at 741741.

You do not have to pretend to be strong. We are reminded in times we feel weak, we are strong. Respect, forgive and love yourself to get support. You are valuable. We need you.

A New Era

She is a prize-winning woman; she carries her trophy with pride because she defeated the odds and rose above the remnants. Sometimes in life, we forget our purpose, we are distracted by the barriers in life. We cannot rise until we fall; we cannot increase until we decrease. In harmony, we can unite in the presence of God and uplift each other. She possesses the land and conquers her enemy; she understands how to write her vision and make it plain, knowing God will not bring you to your valleys without bringing you through, rising above your mountains. Every day, she enters the world with her buckler, shield, helmet and armor. You are somebody! You are a TIN WOMAN with a heart, riding the waves of life until eternity.

May these words empower you with grace to overcome the barriers in life that are keeping you from pursuing your purpose.

Every day, see yourself as a woman with dignity, strength, beauty and integrity. You are only a slave if you allow yourself to become one. I heard your chains fall as you began to unlock the lock. Life is unraveling, like the hands of the clock. Time does not wait; therefore, live life as if today is your… last day.

www.ingramcontent.com/pod-product-compliance
Lightning Source LLC
Chambersburg PA
CBHW060705280326
41933CB00012B/2308